FREDERIK III
The King Who Seized
Absolute Power

by Jens Gunni Busck

Historika

Published in cooperation with the Royal Danish Collection

CONTENTS

Enamel portrait of Frederik III, executed by Paul Prieur in 1663. A masterly example of this painting technique, where the melting point of the enamel determines the number of colours and the size of the portrait, which, with its height of 23 cm, has been stretched to the uttermost.

THE FIRST ABSOLUTE MONARCH

Frederik III (1609–1670) is one of the more mysterious individuals among the Danish kings. This is in part because he was a man who kept his word and seldom committed his intentions to paper but also because of the actual political results he and his queen achieved. Under Frederik III Denmark-Norway became a hereditary absolute monarchy, and both the king's contemporaries and later generations have wondered how a transformation with such profound consequences could occur as suddenly as it did.

It is fairly commonly—but falsely—believed that Danish law has required that the throne be passed from father to son as long as the Danish line of kings has existed. To be sure, this had always been common practice in cases where there were qualified sons who could take over, but before Frederik III's time the monarchy was, strictly speaking, not hereditary. The king had to be chosen, and in the context of the social class system of the Middle Ages this was a task carried out by the ruling class—the nobility. This meant that there was a division of power, and from 1448 onwards—for two centuries—a contract called a håndfæstning was concluded between the Council of the Realm (rigsråd), composed of members of the high nobility and the King. This contract established the limits of the monarch's exercise of power.

When Frederik III became King in 1648, these limits were narrower than ever before. In the context of half a century's power struggles with Christian IV (1577–1648), the Council imposed extraordinarily strict conditions in return for choosing his son to be King. By the time of his death in 1670, Frederik III had become one of Europe's most powerful rulers; the Council of the Realm had been abolished, the nobility had lost a large number of the privileges it had enjoyed up to that point, and the throne was inherited directly by Christian V without an election having taken place previously. Frederik III's male descendants then ruled as absolute monarchs until 1848, though

Painting of the procession that followed the hailing of Frederik III as a hereditary monarch on 18 October 1660. To mark the shift to a hereditary monarchy, Frederik III arranged a splendid ceremony in Copenhagen Castle's square. The sun has broken through the cloud cover and casts its light on the King and the Queen, who are seen on a tribune on the left-hand side with their children. At the far right the Blue Tower can be seen. The castle's square is full of people, and onlookers have climbed the rigging of the ships in the canal. Painted during the years following the coup d'état, probably by Michael van Haven.

The Great Hall at Rosenborg, where three silver lions guard the anointment throne, which was made in the 1660s and is flanked by the throne of the Danish queens, which was made in 1731. The throne was ordered by Frederik III and made by Bendix Grodtschilling of narwhal ivory, which at the time was believed to be unicorn horn. The throne was inspired by that of King Solomon, which, according to the Bible, was made of gold-covered ivory and had six steps, on each of which there were two lions. Frederik III had wished to have a corresponding pride of lions, but the silversmith Ferdinand Küblich only managed to deliver four lions before the King died in 1670, and one of these was melted down and used to make his sarcophagus. Another story, according to which the three lions from the Danish national coat of arms guard the throne, was therefore substituted for the story of King Solomon's twelve lions.

The Judgement of Solomon by Peter Paul Rubens, about 1617. Despite the depleted state coffers during the reign of Frederik III, he was a serious art collector, and this painting is known to have belonged to him. The subject is the biblical story of King Solomon, who is the judge in the case of two women who claim to be the mother of the same child. King Solomon commands his executioner to divide the child in half with a sword so that each woman can have half of the child, whereupon one of the two women is revealed to be the true mother, as she gives up her half to save the child.

several of them had a very difficult time meeting the challenges presented by the responsibilities that came with this position.

The turning point came in 1660, when absolute monarchy was introduced by means of what could justifiably be called a coup d'état. Frederik III's role in this transformation has never been clearly established, but the humiliating defeat that had been suffered by Denmark-Norway just before it took place was a decisive precondition. The so-called Second Northern War, which took place during the years 1655 –1660, not only caused Denmark to lose large territories but also left the country ravaged and impoverished, and Frederik III proved able maximally to exploit a desperate situation when he introduced absolute monarchy without encountering much resistance.

It can be difficult to establish how much influence was wielded by a queen who died long ago, but there is no doubt that Queen Sophie Amalie (1628–1685) made a clear mark on Frederik III's reign. She did not share her husband's tendency to brood silently; on the contrary, she was made to be at the centre of social life and was as extravagant as she was ambitious. While the Queen is surely best known today for her rivalry with Leonora Christina (who was Frederik III's half-sister and married to Corfitz Ulfeldt, who also plays a major role in this story), she certainly left her mark on her age—both because of her fashion sense and because she helped her husband in his struggle for power.

A duke's childhood

Frederik was born on 18 March 1609 at Haderslevhus Castle as the fifth of sixth children born to Christian IV (1577–1648) and Queen Anna Cathrine of Brandenburg

Frederik III's parents, Christian IV and Queen Anna Cathrine, painted in 1612. Two originally separate portraits were sewn together, which is the reason for the rather unusual composition. The figure of the boy is not meant to represent one of the couple's sons but a page.

Duke Frederik, painted by Pieter Isaacsz in 1615. The six-year-old Duke is shown as a musketeer on the training ground, which says a great deal about what was expected of him. With his left hand, he holds a musket on a fork rest and two lit fuses; in the background, Frederiksborg Castle is seen.

(1575–1612). Two sons had been born before him: the firstborn was also named Frederik and died in infancy, while Christian, who was six years older, had been named successor to the throne the previous year and given the title of Prince Elect. Frederik, who was titled Duke Frederik, therefore had no prospects of becoming King of Denmark-Norway, and this did not change until his elder brother died in 1647.

We know only little about Queen Anna Cathrine; she died when Duke Frederik was three years old. All the evidence suggests that she was unable to stand up for herself in relation to her husband, who was an extremely ambitious king whose appetite for life and wealth of initiatives were a constant challenge both to his employees and to his subjects, who were supposed to finance his many projects. Christian IV ruled with a great deal of verve and was at the centre of a courtly culture dominated by masculine values where hunting, gambling, and endless bouts of drinking were core activities. It cannot be said that Duke Frederik followed in his father's footsteps in this regard.

It was also characteristic of Christian IV to display an almost touching amount of interest in his children and was constantly involved in raising them. This was particularly the case where the Chosen Prince was concerned, but he also kept an eye on the younger children and frequently quizzed them on their school subjects. The actual raising of the children was left to trusted employees and took place at various locations outside the home where Frederik received a broad education including Bible studies, languages, writing, rhetoric, mathematics, and music as well as courtly disciplines such as dance and fencing.

It can be assumed that German was a high priority, for at an early stage the little duke was intended to take on a powerful position in Northern Germany. During Frederik's childhood, Christian IV was at the peak of his power and working to secure and expand his territory. He used his children strategically to this end, and in 1621 he succeeded in getting the 12-year-old Frederik chosen as the successor of the bishop in the Bishopric of Bremen. In 1622 he acquired the same status in the neighbouring Bishopric of Verden, where he was made administrator (that is, spiritual ruler) the following year, and in 1624 in Halberstadt as well. With this, the course of Frederik's future was set, though these were waiting positions that for the time being brought no real responsibilities with them.

He still had his education to complete, and during the years 1624–1626 Duke Frederik attended the newly founded Sorø Academy, where he was schooled in subjects including theology, the natural sciences, history, and national law. It was probably during these years that he developed his great appetite for theoretical knowledge, which was not entirely typical of a man whose fate it was to rule.

Bremen and Verden

While Duke Frederik was in Sorø, Christian IV launched a military adventure that became a turning point in his long reign. Kejserkrigen ("the Emperor's War"), as the Danish phase of the Thirty Years' War is called, was motivated by the King's wish to triumph as the defender of the Protestant faith and at the same time outmanoeuvre

The cathedral in Bremen was the prince-archbishop's spiritual seat. Here it is shown flanked by the founders of the Bishopric of Bremen. Painted by Bartholomaeus Bruyn in 1532. During the rule of Duke Frederik, the modest roof structure on the tower to the right collapsed under the weight of the heavy church bells. The tower collapsed in 1638, which cost the lives of eight people who lived in the surrounding houses.

Sweden as a military power. However, a major goal was also the securing of the Northern German prince-bishoprics for Duke Frederik and his younger brother, Duke Ulrik, who had been assigned the Bishopric of Schwerin.

Christian IV entered the war in 1625 as the Duke of Schleswig and Holstein—he had been unable to secure the Council of the Realm's support for his prosecution of the war as King of Denmark-Norway—and the following year he suffered a defeat in the Battle of Lutter (Lutter am Barenberge). When the eighteen-year-old Duke Frederik was made military commander of the Bishopric of Bremen (as the representative of Christian IV, who functioned as a colonel in this connection), the war had in reality been lost. Imperial troops occupied Bremen the following year, and Duke Frederik went to France, where he continued his studies during the years 1629–1630.

Ulrik Frederik Gyldenløve (1638–1704), the son of Duke Frederik and Margrethe Pape, painted by Wolfgang Heimbach in 1661. He distinguished himself during the Second Northern War, and in 1664 he became governor of Norway. He is also known for his marriage to Marie Grubbe, and he made his mark as a builder with projects that included the construction of Charlottenborg in Copenhagen.

After Christian IV it was the Swedes' turn to become involved in the Thirty Years' War, and they achieved a series of victories, including conquering the Bishopric of Bremen in 1632. After the bishopric's administrator died in 1634, however, the Swedish government reluctantly recognized Frederik's claim to Bremen, as the war was going against Sweden by that point. The same year, the Duke was rehabilitated as the administrator of Verden, and after long negotiations with Sweden he was made administrator of Bremen with the title of prince-archbishop. The title did not involve many spiritual duties, so Friedrich II—as he was called in this office—in fact functioned as a secular prince.

For the next ten years, the young prince-bishop ruled under relatively peaceful conditions while the Thirty Years' War continued to rage and the international political situation was generally highly unstable. Internally, these years were characterized by disputes with the various estates that taught Duke Frederik that strong princely power had its advantages.

In 1638 he became a father for the first time when his bourgeois lover Margrethe Pape gave birth to their son Ulrik Frederik Gyldenløve. Naturally, there was no basis for a marriage to Margrethe Pape, so Duke Frederik became engaged to a more appropriate match, the twelve-year-old Sophie Amalie of Brunswick-Lüneburg, the following year.

We know little of Sophie Amalie's childhood; she was born on 24 March 1628 as the only daughter of Duke George of Brunswick, who served with distinction as a general in the Thirty Years' War. She is supposed to have inherited a good share of her father's ambition, and the courtly life that surrounded her during her childhood gave her the well-developed sense of magnificence that would characterize courtly life in Denmark. The wedding took place in October 1643, only a few months before the outbreak of the war that cost Duke Frederik his Northern German territories.

From the war to the throne

Despite the fact that Denmark had prepared for years for a new confrontation with Sweden, it came as a shock when, in December 1643, Swedish troops under General Torstenson marched into Holstein and subsequently occupied Jutland.

Duke Frederik was appointed as a general in the duchies early in 1644, but for a long time he hesitated to lead his troops north to fight the occupying troops in Jutland. He was reluctant to let his prince-bishoprics out of his sight because these also constituted an area of interest to the Swedes. When he did move north late in the year, this did not lead to any remarkable military results, partly because of disputes with the nobleman and marshal Anders Bille, with whose troops Frederik was supposed to combine his own troops in Jutland.

It was therefore necessary to hope for good results from the peace negotiations that were begun in February 1645, but it took time to get Christian IV to accept the occupying power's demands, which included exempting Sweden from the Sound Dues, which were an important source of income for the Danish king. In the meantime the situation worsened, and Duke Frederik had passively to accept that Swedish troops

Duke Frederik's "command rapier from Bremen," which he allegedly used to hack off the arm of a Swedish cavalryman at Ribe during the Torstenson War. In December 1644, Ribe was reconquered by Duke Frederik, who was acting in the capacity of supreme commander of the forces of Schleswig and Holstein. The blade's engraving tells us that the rapier was manufactured by the swordsmith Clemens Dinger in Solingen, Germany.

occupied Bremen and Verden and pushed forward into Schleswig and Holstein. In connection with the subsequent conclusion of peace, the future fate of the bishoprics was made dependent upon negotiations between the prince-bishop who had ruled up to this point and the occupying power, but the Swedes had no interest in giving up these strategically important areas.

Duke Frederik and his young wife now lacked any substantial wealth or land, and in 1646 they settled in Flensburg with financial assistance from Christian IV. For the time being their future was assured by means of a formal division of the coming inheritance from Christian IV between Duke Frederik and the Chosen Prince, but Frederik's brother's health had begun to fail, and when he died without heirs in June 1647 Duke Frederik became the obvious candidate to succeed to the throne of Denmark-Norway. The following month, he formally relinquished his claim to Bremen and Verden, which he could not retain if he wished to become King, and Christian IV gave him an interim position as governor of Schleswig and Holstein.

When Christian IV died at Rosenborg on 28 February 1648, however, the question of the succession to the throne had not yet been resolved. Duke Frederik did not arrive in time to see his father on his deathbed, for the powerful Steward of the Realm, Corfitz Ulfeldt, and his wife, Leonora Christina (the daughter of Christian IV and Kirsten Munk), refrained from having him summoned. This was probably because they were not eager to see the Duke become King, and when he arrived in Copenhagen the following week he was met with broad scepticism by the city's elite. To be sure, Frederik must have seemed like something of a foreigner after his many years in Bremen, but what was more suspicious was that the Duke and his circle of German advisors preferred to see more power wielded by the King than the Danish nobility found acceptable.

Despite the fact that the Steward of the Realm and his wife would have preferred a different outcome, however, Duke Frederik was after all to be the obvious choice of successor. It would not have been easy to break with the tradition of letting the eldest living son succeed to the throne, and it could also not be ignored that as the son of Christian IV the duke had a hereditary right to the royal part of Schleswig and Holstein, which secured the connection between the kingdom and the duchies. The question was how strict the conditions demanded in return for electing him King would be.

Sophie Amalie's hunting set, consisting of a rapier and two knives as well as a monogrammed sheath. The set may have been manufactured in Dresden in the 1640s; the sheath may have been made later. Hunting was one of the Queen's great passions, and above all she loved to hunt swans.

The orb and sceptre
were made by unknown
goldsmiths for the cor-
onation of Frederik III,
where he also wore his
dress sword, which was
probably made by Lu-
cas Schaller in Hamburg
in 1643. The sheath, to
which coats of arms
have been affixed, was
made in Copenhagen
during the period 1666–
1671. After Frederik III's
time, these three splen-
did symbols of power
were used in connection
with the anointing of the
absolute monarchs until
the anointment of Chris-
tian VIII in 1840.

Limited royal power

Contemporaries report that during Duke Frederik's first months in Copenhagen there were heated discussions with his brother-in-law Corfitz Ulfeldt regarding the future division of power between the King and the Council of the Realm. The question also led to long negotiations at a meeting of the nobility in April 1648, but on 7 May Duke Frederik could finally be elected successor, though his power was significantly limited and that of the Council correspondingly strengthened. To put it briefly, the håndfæstning meant that the King could do nothing important without the approval of the Council, not even travel abroad. Duke Frederik's own impact on this power-sharing contract was minimal, but he did manage to get a supplement included that allowed him to retain his German advisors despite a general requirement that the court should consist of Danish nobles.

After having received the title of Prince and Lord of Denmark and Norway and of the Wends and the Goths, the so-called homage—the ceremony in which the subjects kneel before the successor—remained before Frederik could call himself King. The homage took place on 6 July in Copenhagen and on 24 August in Christiania (Oslo). From Norway, Frederik's tour continued to the duchies, where, on 6 October, he was hailed as Archduke of Schleswig and Holstein, after which the royal couple returned home for the two major events that would take place in the capital city in November: Christian IV's funeral on the eighteenth and the coronation five days later.

That about nine months passed before people got around to burying Christian IV was largely due to the fact that Duke Frederik inherited a bankrupt state where there was no money for splendid ceremonies. The state's debt had gotten out of control during the previous years, and faith in the state's ability to pay was practically nonexistent. In this situation it was a challenge even to redeem Christian IV's royal crown, which he had pawned in Hamburg a few years earlier to relieve his desperate financial situation.

A little portrait of Corfitz Ulfeldt decorated with the Order of the Elephant and flanked by an owl holding four playing cards. This is presumably supposed to show that Ulfeldt was a clever fellow with some aces up his sleeve. Eighteenth-century copy based on a portrait type from the 1640s by Karel van Mander.

Frederik III was an enthusiastic collector of books and founded the Royal Library as a private royal collection in 1648. The library grew significantly in the course of the 1660s, when the King bought up a number of the libraries of the nobility, and when he died there were an impressive twenty thousand volumes, some of which bore his monogram. Many of these works had to do with warfare, fortifications, architecture, and the art of governing, but there were also a large number of theological and scientific works. Frederik III was strongly interested in alchemy, which was one of the fashionable sciences of the age, among many other subjects.

The crown was brought home, however, and Frederik III's coronation proceeded more or less as his father's had half a century earlier. Members of the Council of the Realm carried the regalia and assisted in the coronation so that it was symbolically shown that the King received his power from the Council. But on the other hand the absolute monarchy to come was anticipated by Zealand's bishop when he let God and not the nobility grant the right to rule: "The unlimited power God wields over all of the world's kingdoms, this he will share with you as regards the magnificent lands of Denmark and Norway."

Queen Sophie Amalie was crowned the following day, and it was noted during the royal procession through the city that the triumphal arch on Amagertorv had been taken down in the course of the night. It was generally believed that this had been done on the initiative of Corfitz Ulfeldt, whose enmity toward the new King was well-known, but the idea could very well also have come from Ulfeldt's wife, Leonora Christina, who was not prepared to give up her position as First Lady of the court. The Queen had to tolerate the insult, however, for the simple reason that the coronation festivities would hardly have taken place if Ulfeldt had not provided collateral for a large part of the expenses.

The new royal couple and their children—at the time they had their son Christian (V) and their daughter Anna Sophie and had a new baby on the way—moved into Frederiksborg Palace with their German-speaking court. Limited in his power as he was, Frederik III bided his time at first and left governing to Corfitz Ulfeldt and Chancellor Christian Thomesen Sehested, who had primary responsibility for the håndfæstning, in particular.

Queen Sophie Amalie dressed as a farm girl, painted by Wolfgang Heimbach in about 1650. Dressing up in costumes was popular at the court, where festivals often had themes. The farmer theme was something special because it eradicated differences in rank for as long as the festival lasted, which allowed for a greater degree of abandon and for unusual social relationships. Sophie Amalie was an eager ballet dancer, and she is known to have performed dances as a farm girl on several occasions.

Ivory model of the frigate Norske Løve ("the Norwegian Lion"), carved during the years 1652–1654. Frederik III had a sure sense of art and craftsmanship, and when the ivory carver Jacob Jensen gave the new King some samples of his skill during the King's visit to Norway in 1648, Frederik III hired him on the spot. The ship model is Jacob Jensen's magnum opus and features countless amazing details. Boiling ivory made it possible to use this material even for the sails.

The fall of the brothers-in-law

At the beginning of Frederik's reign, Corfitz Ulfeldt and Leonora Christina practically appeared to be the kingdom's first couple in the capital city. In the course of the 1640s, Ulfeldt had amassed a fortune by means of methods that were not entirely legal, and the couple manifested a cosmopolitan elegance that was unrivalled in Denmark.

Ulfeldt was also a diplomat who could achieve results, so in 1649 Frederik III agreed to send the Steward of the Realm and his wife to the Netherlands to establish a Danish-Dutch defensive alliance. Ulfeldt achieved his goal and also concluded a new customs agreement for Dutch ships passing through the Øresund, but his return home did not turn out to be the triumphal procession he had imagined. Power shifts at court and new internal alliances had considerably reduced his influence in the meantime, so the Steward of the Realm chose to take to his sickbed as he liked to do when things went against him.

Within the Council of the Realm and the nobility, there was widespread hostility toward both the power-hungry Steward of the Realm and the King's other prominent brother-in-law, Hannibal Sehested, who was the governor of Norway. Frederik III was able to exploit this envy, and it no doubt pleased many that the King stopped referring to his half-sisters as Countesses of Schleswig and Holstein and began calling his own daughters princesses rather than damsels simply to underscore his half-sisters' non-royal status. Another insult was that Frederik III forbade the sisters to drive into the courtyard of Copenhagen Castle, so when the royal couple's third daughter, Princess Wilhelmine Ernestine, was to be baptized in October 1650 Leonora Christina demonstratively stayed away.

A few months later, the Steward of the Realm was involved in a strange drama when a lady of questionable reputation, Dina Vinhofvers, went to the court and claimed to be Ulfeldt's lover and pregnant with his child. She claimed that she had heard the Ulfeldts talk about poisoning the King, and the intrigue became truly absurd when Dina subsequently went to the Steward of the Realm and his wife and told them that she also knew of a plan to do away with them. When Frederik III offered to have the couple's home placed under guard and Ulfeldt declined this offer, the King had to see this as an indirect accusation that he was behind the alleged murder plot. The whole matter was based on verbal claims rather than hard evidence, but for months it was the big topic of conversation in the capital city, where mutual suspicions and accusations flew back and forth. The end of it was that Dina—who was doubtless a pawn in the games of others—was executed for perjury. While Ulfeldt was acquitted, the matter weakened him and paved the way for Frederik III's next move.

During the summer of 1651, the King asked the Council again to take a position on a number of accusations of fraud and corruption in Ulfeldt's administration that had been presented earlier, and these accusations, in contrast to those heard in relation to the alleged murder plot, were founded on facts. The Steward of the Realm and his wife wisely chose to flee the country, and a few months later they settled in Sweden—of all places!—where they soon gained influence at the court.

Just a few weeks previously, Hannibal Sehested had lost his offices. The enterprising governor had actually been on good terms with Frederik III but had made enemies on the Council by implementing reforms in Norway that had reduced Danish income from there. Sehested had also enriched himself at the Crown's expense, in part via bribery deals with suppliers to the state, and on this basis a number of charges were brought to which the governor unwisely responded by delivering a confession that was partly in written form. The result was that Sehested was forced to repay a staggering amount of money and give up his offices.

While Frederik III would have liked to have kept Sehested, the fall of the two brothers-in-law, seen in retrospect, was a step on the path toward absolute monarchy. The Council of the Realm lost its two most capable individuals and thus weakened itself as an institution, which made it more difficult to fill the supremely dominant position the Council had assigned itself via the håndfæstning. As is well-known, it is cold at the top, and in the following years the provincial nobility and the lower classes came to view the Council with increasing animosity and criticism, while the King was able to increase his influence slowly but steadily.

Frederik III's five eldest children. Enamel portrait executed by Paul Prieur in 1671 on the basis of a painting from 1652 that is now lost. Crown Prince Christian (V), in blue, draws his bow while his sisters watch in admiration. The youngest, Prince Frederik, tugs at Princess Anna Sophia's basket of flowers.

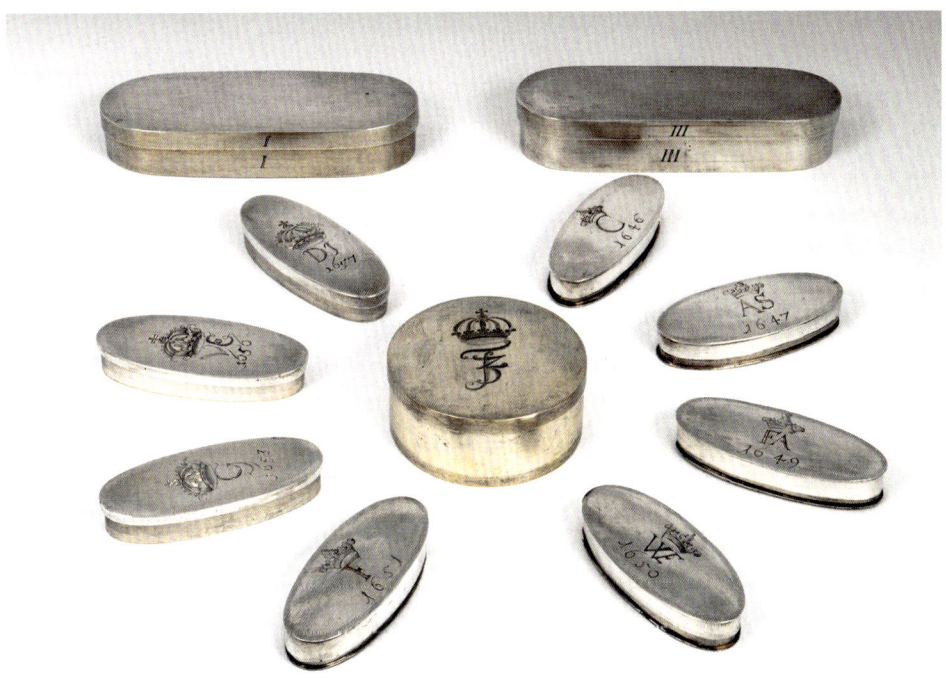

The expenses of the state

During all the power struggles of the 1650s, the nearly empty coffers of the state constituted a constant problem. At the beginning of the decade, a sale of state-owned land took place, and this reduced state debt by one-fourth, but it was not easy to generate steady income. The introduction of a new consumption tax on beer and strong spirits was one of the more effective measures, but it increased the dissatisfaction of the bourgeoisie with the privileges of the nobility and the clergy, as these estates were exempt from taxes and fees.

An important measure was making the administration of the customs system more effective, and various projects were launched to promote business activity. However, the city found itself in a severe depression, which was not improved when the islands and particularly Copenhagen were ravaged by plague in 1654. About a third of the population of the capital city died while the elite remained at a safe distance; Frederik

Nine silver boxes, eight of which contain the umbilical cords of the children Frederik III had by Sophie Amalie—three boys and five girls. Umbilical cords were believed to protect people against illness and death. In the box in the centre is Frederik III's amniotic—his "victory shirt"—which was unbroken when he was born, which was seen as a sign of strength and victory.

III and his family, which now included five children, moved with the court to the palace Flensborghus, where they stayed for more than a year.

The surviving inhabitants of Copenhagen did enjoy more space, for the area of the city was more than doubled during these years. Christian IV had laid out the plans for the city expansion, and now robust fortifications were built that ran from Nørreport to Sankt Annæ Skanse (St. Anne's Redoubt, later the Citadel). At the same time, diligent work was being done to build fortresses in Scania, Nakskov, and Glückstadt, and not least at the Little Belt, where the royal couple gave their names to the double fortress of Sofieodde (Funen) and Frederiksodde (Jutland). The latter fortress was renamed Fredericia in 1664. The fortifications were important because it was difficult to build up an effective defensive army. The state simply could not afford mercenary troops, and creating an effective force consisting of conscripted farmers was a major challenge.

Given that the Torstenson War was well remembered, there were limits on how much one could save on defence, but some people found the expenses incurred by courtly life to be overly extravagant. The magnificence of the court was certainly not exaggerated by international standards, but Frederik III did not tend to deny his young queen anything, and Queen Sophie Amalie liked nothing better than being the shining centre of a festival.

Under the leadership of Sophie Amalie, the court realized the ideals of the Baroque period to a hitherto unseen degree; educated conversation and formally correct behaviour were given a high priority that contrasted starkly with what had been the case in the age of Christian IV. It was an innovation that French culture became firmly established at the court, where speaking French became a sign that one had been properly educated, though German was also spoken. The preference for French quickly spread to the nobility and the bourgeoisie, who tried to live up to the royal example as best they could.

The court's large-scale spending was not just an expression of snobbery and pleasure-seeking; it served a political purpose. The pompous splendour strengthened the prestige of the monarchy—and thus of the royal couple—and at the same time could give foreign powers the impression that things were going better for the Danish-Norwegian realm than they actually were.

Portrait of Sophie Amalie with a parrot on her hand. The artist cannot be identified, but the style points in the direction of the Dutch painter Juriaen Ovens. In the process of restoration a few years ago it was revealed that the left arm was first painted hanging down, so the parrot was later added as an exotic element to pep the portrait up.

Frederik III and Sophie Amalie mounted and surrounded by flowers. Probably painted by Ottmar Elliger in about 1655. The composition gives a romantic impression of the couple's life together, and this impression was presumably still justified by reality when the picture was painted.

The Second Northern War

Few thought that the Danish-Swedish conflict had reached its actual resolution with the Torstenson War, and Frederik III had not given up the thought of reconquering Bremen and Verden.

While Denmark-Norway was poorly prepared militarily, interesting perspectives opened up in 1656, when Russia and the Netherlands united to support the Polish troops against Sweden, which had invaded Poland the previous year. The government in Copenhagen was asked to join the efforts against Sweden, and Frederik III tried to launch a military buildup by addressing the Council of the Realm repeatedly in this connection, but the Council was hesitant. When a meeting of the estates of the realm was called in February 1657, resistance to going to war proved to be limited, and after Sweden had launched a new offensive in Poland the King and the Council decided to declare war.

The royal couples from a chess set featuring Danes and Swedes, carved in limestone after Frederik III was defeated by Charles X Gustav in 1658. The Danish Queen wears a crown, the Swedish, in contrast, only a hat, which is a reference to Leonora Christina, who was known for wearing a hat and had gone over to the Swedish side.

The prosecution of the war by Denmark-Norway had the unmistakable character of an act of revenge. A main force was sent to Bremen-Verden, and attempts were made to reconquer Halland as well as Jämtland and Härjedalen in Norway, which had been respectively pawned and lost in the Torstenson War. Only the Norwegian action was successful. The campaign in Germany proceeded according to plan, but the Swedish king Charles X Gustav reacted resolutely and moved west with a force of thirteen thousand men, after which the Danes retreated. The Swedish force reached Holstein in late July, conquered both duchies in August, and on 24 October took the newly built fortress of Frederiksodde, which was the most important bastion in Jutland.

Toward the end of 1657 everyone thought the war had been put on hold for the winter, but now the curtain went up on an unusual episode in military history. The winter was so cold that the Danish Belts froze, and Charles X Gustav dared to send

his troops across the ice. On 30 January, the Swedish army crossed the Little Belt, and a week later it crossed the Great Belt, reaching Lolland via Langeland—despite the fact that the temperature had been above freezing for the previous few days! This was a courageous and risky move by the Swedish king, but the ice held. After this the Swedish troops were able to march to Copenhagen without difficulty, and with the enemy outside the gates of the capital city Frederik III and the Council were forced to surrender. The result was the bitterest defeat in Denmark-Norway's history, and the Swedes chose no lesser personage than Corfitz Ulfeldt to lead the negotiations. He had accompanied the Swedish forces all the way on their passage across the Belts and now took the most spectacular revenge one could imagine. At the conclusion of the Treaty of Roskilde, which was signed on 11 February 1658, Denmark had to give up Scania, Halland, and Blekinge as well as Bohuslän and Trondheim in Norway.

Charles X Gustav subsequently began a campaign aimed at Prussia, but in the course of the summer he gave in to the temptation to give the Danish state the coup de grâce. In early August 1658, a powerful army took ship at Kiel. Two days later this army landed at Korsør, and shortly thereafter it had surrounded Copenhagen. The city was not prepared to surrender, however, and because the Swedes did not control the Øresund it was possible to supply the city by sea. Furthermore, the Danish-Dutch defensive alliance now became a factor, because Sweden was the aggressor, and in late October a Dutch fleet arrived with three thousand troops and large amounts of supplies.

The other European powers were not prepared to allow a Swedish empire to dominate the entire Nordic region, and the same year forces from Brandenburg and Poland as well as imperial forces marched into the duchies and on up into Jutland, where the Swedes were forced to retreat—though of course they ravaged and burned as much as possible to destroy the advancing army's potential provisions. To the populace, the advancing "liberators" turned out to be an even greater scourge than the Swedish troops had been, and thousands died of disease and hunger as a result of the army's behaviour.

The night of 10/11 February 1659, the Swedes finally dared an attack on Copenhagen, but it was a total fiasco, resulting in only twelve dead on the Danish side in contrast to at least 580 Swedes. After this Charles X Gustav had to abandon his ambition of achieving a total military victory, but there continued to be intense fighting for dom-

Page 31:
The assault on Copenhagen on 11 February 1659. Frederik III's conduct during the fighting contributed to securing the support that rendered him able to push through the implementation of absolute monarchy.

The Battle of Nyborg on 14 November 1659 is seen as one of the decisive Danish victories during the second phase of Denmark's conflict with Sweden's King Charles X Gustav (1658–1660). That fall, Swedish-occupied Funen was transformed into a battlefield when Danish and allied troops attacked from opposite sides, and the Battle of Nyborg ended with the Swedes having to surrender their fortress. This portrait was painted by Wolfgang Heimbach in 1659 and shows Frederik III kneeling during the battle after an angel has appeared to him. In fact the King was not present at Nyborg at all.

ination of the Danish islands, and Lolland, Falster, Møn, and Langeland ended up under Swedish control.

Funen was reconquered in the fall of 1659 with the help of Denmark-Norway's allies, and after this the main struggle took place in Norway, where the Swedes launched an offensive around New Year's Day 1660. But in February Charles X Gustav died after having been ill for a few days, and with this the driving force behind the aggressive Swedish military policies was eliminated. A few days later the Swedish military campaign was called off and peace negotiations could begin.

When a peace treaty was concluded in May 1660, Bornholm and Trondheim were returned to Denmark-Norway, but the Danish areas east of the Øresund remained Swedish spoils of war. The treaty was the result of English, Dutch, and French mediation and showed who was in control in Europe. There was a desire to ensure that Denmark-Norway could continue to constitute a counterweight to Sweden but a willingness to allow Sweden to move its border to the Øresund. Strictly speaking, this eliminated the geographic justification for the Sound Dues, but Denmark's right to demand the dues was nevertheless secured and remained in force until 1857.

The coup d'état

The foreign troops left Denmark in poor condition. The population had been reduced significantly, particularly as a result of famine and plague that had followed the troops around the country. The physical destruction was so great that it would take decades to rebuild the country.

Though Frederik III bore a significant share of the responsibility for provoking the war, he appeared in a much more positive light than the Council of the Realm when blame was assigned. It was reasonable to blame the Council for the lack of military preparedness at the beginning of the war, but later, too, there was a tendency to give the King the honour for everything that went well, while the nobility were blamed for the defeats.

Part of the reason for this was to be found in historical tradition, for the nobility, as a warrior class, had been exempt from taxes for centuries and could therefore be held accountable—despite the fact that the nobility had made a major contribution to the war effort. But events that had transpired behind Copenhagen's fortifications during

Mother-of-pearl portrait of Frederik III, probably made by Jeremias Hercules in about 1665. Small pieces of mother-of-pearl in various hues are inlaid in slate in a metal frame.

nearly two years of siege had also played a decisive role. In contrast to many nobles, Frederik III chose to remain in the city during the siege; he had responded to being urged to flee with a relevant quote from the Book of Job, "I shall die in my nest!" The royal couple frequently showed themselves on the walls, where they encouraged the work on the defences, and while the city was besieged an unusual community and cooperation across the classes developed with the King as its common point of reference. During the attack on Copenhagen Frederik III had been present at the most vulnerable locations, so he enjoyed massive support in the capital after the siege.

In addition, the Council was weakened after having lost Chancellor Christian Thomesen Sehested and Rigsmarsk (Marshal) Anders Bille, the King's old enemy, who had died after having been wounded at Frederiksodde, in 1657. Frederik III had been in no hurry to appoint their successors, and with the establishment of a new council of war during the winter of 1657–1658 the King had in reality taken control of the armed forces. This would prove to be important.

When a meeting of the estates of the realm was called in 1660, the primary purpose was alleviating the serious financial crisis, for the state had incurred bottomless debt to finance the wars, and the occupation of Denmark, which had lasted almost three years, had blocked most tax and customs income. When the estates of the realm gathered in Copenhagen in September 1660, it was therefore quickly agreed that the army should be reduced in size and a consumption tax should be introduced, as the Council proposed.

It was new, however, that the burghers refused to let the nobility be exempted from paying the tax as was traditional, and it was also a new phenomenon that the burghers allied themselves with the clergy and presented a number of common proposals. The most radical of these was presented on 4 October and read as follows: "... that we wish to recognize His Royal Majesty as our most merciful lord and king and all His Majesty's heirs as the proper heirs to the realm." In other words, it was proposed that the electoral monarchy be replaced by a hereditary monarchy.

This was a revolutionary proposal, for if a hereditary right to rule was established, then the King would no longer need to be elected, and the opportunity to make demands in this connection would thus be eliminated. The Council and the nobility were not prepared to give up their power by approving such a decisive legal change, of course, so on 10 October its proponents went directly to the King and presented their proposal. Given the constraints established by the håndfæstning, Frederik III could do

Next spread:
The hailing of Fredcrik III as a hereditary king in the square in front of Copenhagen Castle on 18 October 1660. The scene was painted by the deaf-mute Wolfgang Heimbach, who can be seen swinging his hat at the bottom left. It took him six years to complete this painting. The sunbeam breaking through the clouds to touch the Lord's chosen one is characteristic of the absolute monarchy's new self-image.

no more than demand a response from the Council of the Realm and the nobility by the following day, but to render the decision easier to make he imposed martial law. The same evening, the number of guards posted in the city was doubled, and the next morning the ports and the harbour were closed so the nobility could not sabotage the meeting of the estates of the realm by leaving the city. Frederik III now had a decisive advantage because he had taken control of the armed forces during the war, and the Council and the nobility could do nothing but accept a transformation of the state.

After a few days of negotiations between the King and the Council, the representatives of the estates of the realm appeared at Copenhagen Castle on 13 October and offered Frederik III the hereditary right to the crown for himself and his descendants. It was still necessary to clarify which rules would replace the håndfæstning, however, and the estates of the realm could not get anywhere near reaching an agreement. The consequence of this was that they simply gave up and left it to the King to create a new constitution. With this the estates of the realm had not only freed Frederik III from all the conditions he had accepted in 1648 but also given him free hands with regard to defining the political ground rules that would apply in the future.

On 18 October, Frederik III let himself be hailed as a hereditary king at a hastily arranged ceremony in which he secured promises of loyalty from the estates of the realm and the Council. The foundation of a new political system had thus been established, and this had occurred in a surprisingly orderly fashion. There were no notable protests subsequently, either, which in itself can be seen as a testimony to the fact that a change in the system had been necessary.

Who took the initiative in presenting the proposal remains something of a mystery, however. There is no doubt that Frederik III was eager to see the hereditary right to rule established, and there were connections between the court and the lower classes, which had a common interest in breaking the power of the high nobility. But the agreements were reached behind closed doors, and no minutes of these meetings were kept, so historians have never established a clear answer to this question.

The consolidation of absolute power

The common people hardly saw many signs that a change in the system had taken place in Copenhagen, for life went on in the villages and in the houses in the mar-

The Citadel in Copenhagen is closely connected to the introduction of absolute monarchy. This fortification, which is still well-preserved, was built during the years 1662–1664 as an expansion of Christian IV's Sankt Annæ Skanse (St. Anne's Redoubt) and follows the European norm of the age for five-pointed fortifications. There were plans to build an entire little Baroque military town within the walls, but this ended up being too expensive to become a reality. This plan included a castle to which the King could retire in case of war or revolt against the absolute monarchy. Frederik III knew that a revolt against the new form of government was a possibility, and some held his distrust of his subjects against him. The gates and the characteristic red barracks are from Frederik III's time, and the city is the world's oldest still-functioning military complex.

Peder Schumacher Griffenfeld (1635–1699), painted by Paul Prieur in 1675. Young Peder Schumacher was the first individual of bourgeois origin who exploited the new opportunities available under the absolute monarchy. He entered Frederik III's service in 1662 as the head of the Royal Library and Archive, and as the King's personal secretary he became the main author of the Royal Law and therewith a driving force in the construction of the absolute monarchy's administration. After the death of Frederik III, he managed to become Great Chancellor of the realm before falling out of the graces of Christian V in 1676. He spent most of the remainder of his life in prison.

ket towns, where the struggle to survive was hard despite the fact that the war was over. One can also question how great a social change the coup d'état in fact represented, for the introduction of absolute monarchy had been made possible by a gradual centralization and strengthening of state power that had been ongoing for a long time. However, the transformation of the state did mean that one power elite (the King and his circle) pushed another (the noblemen of the Council) away from the centre of power, and this made it possible for Frederik III to push through a number of reforms that secured the new form of government for the future and simultaneously strengthened the central state power. Only the most important of these changes are described below.

New privileges

In January 1661, Frederik III composed the so-called Absolute Government Act, which defined the new form of government and added absolute power to the hereditary right to rule he had already been granted. Those who had desired a system in which the power of the King continued to be limited by various instances (such as the meetings of the estates of the realm) were thus bitterly disappointed; the King now possessed supreme power.

Frederik III acted in accordance with widespread expectations when, in June 1661, he granted the estates—the nobility, the clergy, and the burghers—their new privileges. The fears of the nobility were justified, for they lost their old exemption from taxes, which was now dependent on the King's goodwill. At the same time, noblemen were exempted for a period of ten years from their duty to perform military service in wartime, but with this the old concept of nobility became empty, for traditionally nobility had been based on this: exemption from taxes in return for military service. And while up to now it had been nearly impossible for non-nobility to become peers, the King now took for himself the unlimited right to grant peerages, which was a small revolution in itself.

The other estates benefited from changes implemented by the King. The burghers of Copenhagen had their special privileges confirmed; these privileges had been promised to the burghers by Frederik III as a means of motivating the defensive efforts during the siege. The remainder of the burghers of the realm and the clergy were granted a number of lesser benefits and no longer limited by their previous status as "unfree estates," which theoretically gave them access to the realm's highest positions, if they were adequately qualified.

Ring of enamelled gold with diamonds. This tasteful ring featuring a penis and a woman's hand may have been a gift from Frederik III to his wife after it was discovered in 1664 that the Queen had had an affair with her valet.

Sophie Amalienborg, which was the predecessor of today's Amalienborg, was a magnificent Italian-inspired villa that was built for the Queen in the years around 1670. The palace burned down in 1689, when a temporary theatre that had been built for the occasion of Christian V's forty-fourth birthday celebration caught fire. More than two hundred people—mostly children—died in the fire, and Sophie Amalie lost a beautiful architectural legacy.

Wax bust of Queen Sophie Amalie, attributed to Antoine Benoist, probably made in about 1670. It was made by using a plaster cast and is therefore a closer approximation of reality than many painted portraits. Wax portraits were a fashionable phenomenon of the time; their popularity had spread from the court of Louis XIV in France.

Finally, the "royal officers" received their own privileges. These officers constituted the new non-noble bureaucracy, which became an estate for itself with a special legal status and the same rights with regard to land ownership as those enjoyed by the nobility. There was a strategy behind this: by granting these special rights, the King bound the bureaucrats to himself in a special relationship characterized by loyalty and dependency.

Administrative reforms

In the early 1660s, Frederik III secured absolute monarchy for the future by implementing administrative changes that were so extensive that it became practically impossible to return to the old system, and a major innovation was the creation of so-called colleges for the various administrative areas. These consisted of both burghers and noblemen and had the purpose of making expertise and administrative capacity available to the King. The college system was intended to ensure that the King received qualified recommendations on the basis of which he could make his sovereign decisions as well as to ensure that these decisions were carried out. The Supreme Court was established in 1661, also in accordance with this model. It was more or less a continuation of the Council of the Realm as far as the former Council's judicial function was concerned; the former members of the Council were given seats here.

Another measure was the transformation of the old fiefs into new administrative units, amter, which constituted an attack on the dominant position in local administration that had been enjoyed by the lensmand (sheriff) up to this point. The new administrative officials, the amtsmænd, were also noblemen but were hired by the King and received a fixed salary, and this put more money in the central coffers of the realm. Further, the King arranged for better control over the towns; in Denmark, towns received so-called magistracies (city councils) and were thus placed under the central administration in Copenhagen.

In the midst of all the new measures, the abysmal financial crisis of the early 1660s was a colossal problem, for state debt was even greater than it had been in 1648. Frederik III chose the same solution that had been chosen back then, namely selling state-owned land. During the following years, about a third of the crown lands were sold, but while these sales put money in the state's coffers in the short term, they also reduced the state's ongoing receipt of revenues. This made the state more dependent on collecting taxes, customs duties, and fees—which made it even more necessary to have effective centralized administration.

The Lex Regia

In connection with the transformation of the state, Frederik III had promised a new law that would replace the scrapped håndfæstning as the basis of the state's political life. The new privileges of the estates had partially fulfilled this promise, but there was still a need for a replacement for the parts of the håndfæstning that had established constitutional law. Five years passed before there was such a replacement: the Royal Law of 1665, which was primarily the work of a brilliant young man, Peder Schumacher (later Griffenfeld).

Both in form and content, the Royal Law was the constitution of absolute monarchy, and it functioned as such until 1848. In an international context, this was a unique phenomenon, for no other absolutist regimes have had a written constitution, neither before the creation of the Royal Law nor since. In contrast to the håndfæstninger that had existed previously, and in contrast to the constitution of 1049, the Royal Law was not a constitution that regulated a division of power; on the contrary, it established that power was indivisible and collected in the person of the King. The law established the rules for the peaceful transferral of power from king to king, and above all it established the ideological basis for the regime's exercise of power.

In the introduction the transferral of power in 1660 is described as voluntary and as an expression of God's will, and the new type of state is thereafter defined as a "hereditary absolute monarchy" that is to exist as long as there are descendants in Frederik III's royal line. The text of the law itself establishes that the King is answerable only to God and not bound by any law created by men—except the Royal Law—and that for this reason he can introduce, rewrite, and nullify laws as he wishes. The King is the source of the law itself, just as he is the source of all official power and for this reason has the right to appoint officers to all offices. It is also established that the King has the right to take up arms (that is, he has a monopoly on the right to use violence) and is the head of the church and as such is to ensure that his subjects observe the correct Protestant faith. The ideological basis of the Royal Law, however, is not religion but natural law: the legitimacy of the absolute monarch is based on the fact that his subjects have transferred power to him in their own best interests.

The Lex Regia was signed by Frederik III on 14 November 1665. The law contains provisions regarding the priority of hereditary succession, the ruler's church affiliation, and the indivisibility of the realm, but otherwise the King is granted unlimited authority. The Royal Law was replaced by the Constitutional Act of Denmark (Danmarks Riges Grundlov) in 1849, but the rules of hereditary succession were not nullified until the Law on Succession to the Throne took effect in 1853.

The so-called Marble Room at Rosenborg was originally the bedroom of Christian IV's second wife, Kirsten Munk. In 1668, Frederik III had the room refurbished in a pompous Baroque style; the ceiling was covered with new plaster, and the walls were covered with artificial marble, probably created by the Italian stucco worker Francesco Bruno. On the ceiling there are paintings of putti, that is, small chubby angel-like child figures, who are carrying the regalia; in the heart-shaped areas surrounding the picture the individual components of the coat of arms of the realm have been painted.

Despite the fact that the contents of the Royal Law could hardly have shocked people to the same degree that the signing of the agreement transferring all power to the King or the bestowal of the new privileges could have, the law was hidden away as a state secret after it had been signed. It was read at the coronation of Christian V in 1671 but not published in written form until 1709.

A rocket burns out

Frederik III died of pneumonia on 9 February 1670 at Copenhagen Castle. Shortly before his death, he had written the following words:

"In my life, I was comparable to a rocket that rises into the air and shines beautifully and clearly the moment it is lit; but when I had reached the highest point and glittered like a thousand stars, an explosion was heard, and immediately I disappeared before the eyes of the onlookers, fell to earth, and became dust and ashes."

It is interesting that Frederik III, who was otherwise introspective and a man of few words, could summarize his life with a metaphor of glittering before onlookers. However, the statement fits well within the frame of a French-oriented courtly culture, in which self-confident behaviour was often coupled with keeping life at an ironic distance. The image seems to indicate that during his rapidly progressing illness Frederik III could look back on his life as a successful whole.

Queen Sophie Amalie was hardly burdened by sorrow, for the couple had drifted apart in the previous ten years. After the couple had experienced their great common triumph, the introduction of absolute monarchy, the Queen lost influence, for Frederik III increasingly sought advice and guidance from people with whom Sophie Amalie was at odds. Furthermore, the Royal Law ended up containing provisions with regard to inheritance to which the Queen was strongly opposed, and in fact by the late 1660s she considered her position to have become so threatened that she feared an assassination attempt.

Despite her reduced influence, Queen Sophie Amalie did not let herself be limited by attempts to save money now, either. In 1661, she had had the palace Dronninggård built on the lake Furesø; this palace was the setting of many lavish Baroque festivals. In 1669–1673, Sophie Amalienborg was built as a replacement for her

This large painting by Heinrich Dittmer, which depicts Frederik III on his deathbed, hangs in Roskilde Cathedral. A delegation of pompous angels strews flowers over the King and confirms his God-given absolute power by laying a crown on his head.

Dowager Queen Sophie Amalie, portrayed by Abraham Wuchters in about 1675. As a widow, too, Sophie Amalie strove to gain as much power as possible, and she openly competed with Christian V's queen Charlotte Amalie for precedence at court. Her eldest son ultimately freed himself from her influence entirely, which must have been made easier by the fact that Sophie Amalie favoured her next-eldest son, Prince Jørgen, whom she attempted to make her sole heir.

earlier pleasure palace, Dronningens Enghave, which had been destroyed during the Swedish siege.

The legacy

On Frederik III's coffin in Roskilde Cathedral is a pompous epitaph that begins with the following words: "Here lies the man to whom Denmark owes its survival." While it

The painter Christian Zahrtmann was influenced by Leonora Christina's Jammers Minde (literally "a history of lament," translated into English as Memoirs of Leonora Christina), when, in 1882, he depicted the death of Sophie Amalie; in the painting, the ugly old woman has only Christian V with her. She is alleged to be whispering to him, as her last wish, that Leonora Christina must not be released. There is some doubt as to whether the Queen's hatred of her former rival was indeed that long-lasting, but Zahrtmann was convinced and painted many pictures based on Jammers Minde in which Leonora Christina was depicted as dignified, frugal, and motherly.

was mostly the interests of the great European powers that secured Denmark's survival, it is correct that for Denmark-Norway the Second Northern War was a struggle for survival, and the importance of Frederik III's actions during the war should not be underestimated.

The King's stoic remark that he would die in his nest, made while the Swedish army was marching toward the capital, is the kind of quote that can create a legacy. This supremely well-chosen remark would become a standing argument for absolute monarchy, and with time it was absorbed into the national mythology, where it is not very important that the Swedish army's march across the ice went via the Belts and not over the Øresund as some versions of the story have it.

The otherwise splendid legacy left by Frederik III and Queen Sophie Amalie suffered serious damage; however, in 1869, when Leonora Christina's memoir Jammers Minde (literally "a memory of lament," translated into English as Memoirs of Leonora Christina) was published. The King's half-sister had spent twenty-two years as a prisoner in the Blue Tower in Copenhagen Castle after having been abducted in England in 1663, and she felt an understandable bitterness towards the King and especially the Queen that, to put it mildly, was expressed in her manuscript, which had been hidden away for almost two hundred years. While it was later established that Leonora Christina's account should be taken with a pinch of salt, the literary quality is undeniable, and the book immediately became a success. Sophie Amalie was thus cast in the role of an outright villain. A few years previously, on the other hand, she and Frederik III had been the subjects of a far more flattering—though less reliable—depiction in Carit Etlar's entertaining 1853 novel Gøngehøvdingen (The Gønge Chieftain). For generations of Danes, this account of the deeds of Svend Poulsen was a definitive story of the Second Northern War.

The fact that Frederik III is not remembered to the same extent as his colourful predecessor has something to do with his personality but is also due in part to what he left behind. The legacy of Frederik III was in particular a new form of state, but this was abolished in 1849, and in contrast to Christian IV he did not create cities and impressive buildings that could keep his memory alive. However, the fortifications around central Fredericia are still standing today, and the Citadel in Copenhagen is a well-preserved monument to the establishment of the absolute monarchy and has Frederik III's monogram chiselled into the stone above the gates.

Something else that would have pleased him is that the Royal Library still exists and the Art Chamber's function is preserved by the special museums to which its collections were transferred in the nineteenth century. While Frederik III remains a mystery to us, we know this was a legacy that was important to him.

The Art Chamber building was built on Slotsholmen during the years 1665–1673. One of Copenhagen's earliest Baroque buildings, it was inspired by French buildings and built as a home for both the Art Chamber and the Royal Library, which in the 1660s was led by Peter Schumacher Griffenfeld (Whose statue is seen from the back). The Art Chamber was founded around 1650 by Frederik III, and after his reign the collection grew rapidly. When the Art Chamber was closed down in 1825, the collection was transferred to other sites including the National Museum and the treasure chamber at Rosenborg.

SUGGESTIONS FOR FURTHER READING

Thomas Lyngby / Søren Mentz / Sebastian Olden-Jørgensen: *Magt og Pragt – Enevælde 1660–1848,* Gads Forlag 2010.
A book that provides basic information regarding the Danish absolute monarchy; it describes both the exercise and staging of power and offers a broad perspective on the rest of Europe during this period.

Steffen Heiberg: *Enhjørningen Corfitz Ulfeldt,* Gyldendal 2003.
An engaging book about Denmark's most iconic traitor. This is a scholarly biography, but it is as entertaining as a novel.

Leonora Christina: *Memoires of Leonora Christina, Daughter of Christian IV of Denmark.* Forgotten Books 2015.
The masterpiece that gave Leonora Christina a posthumous triumph over her old enemies.

Knud J.V. Jespersen: *Danmarks historie bind 3 [volume 3] – Tiden 1648–1730,* Gyldendal 1898.
A reference work giving an overview of the period that includes the reign of Frederik III and of sources. Also recommended: Ståle Dyrvik: Truede tvillingriker 1648–1720, volume III of the series Danmark-Norge 1380–1814, Universitetsforlaget 1998.

Roskildefreden 1658 – i perspektiv, Roskilde Museums Forlag 2009.
A fine little anthology of texts concerning the Treaty of Roskilde, the events that led to it, and its significance as a factor contributing to the establishment of absolute monarchy.

Jørgen Hein: *The Treasure Collection at Rosenborg Castle I-III,* Museum Tusculanum 2009.
A splendid publication in three volumes about the collection in the treasure chamber at Rosenborg Palace.

www.kongernessamling.dk.

Frederik III
The King Who Seized Absolute Power

Copyright © 2016
The Royal Danish Collection and Historika / Gads Forlag A/S

ISBN: 978-87-93229-38-9
First edition, first print run

Printed in Lithuania

Text: Jens Gunni Busck
Edited by Axel Harms
Translated from Danish by Peter Sean Woltemade
Cover and graphic design Lene Nørgaard, Propel
Printed by Clemenstrykkeriet, Lithuania

Illustrations:
Front page, p. 2, 4, 9, 15, 16, 17, 19, 21, 22, 24, 25, 26, 28, 31, 32, 35, 36, 38-39, 42, 44, 45, 46, 48-49, 52, 56-57: The Royal Danish Collection, p. 6-7: Jens Markus Lindhe, p. 8: Statens Museum for Kunst, p. 10: Det Nationalhistoriske Museum på Frederiksborg Slot (photo: Lennart Larsen), p. 13: Det Nationalhistoriske Museum på Frederiksborg Slot (photo: Kit Weiss), p. 12, 41: Scanpix, p. 18, 43: Iben Bølling Kaufmann, p. 20: Det Kongelige Bibliotek, p.29: Malmö Museer (photo: Lena Wilhelmson), p. 30: Korshunova/Dreamstime.com, p. 50: Roskilde Domsogns Arkiv, p. 53: Den Hirschprungske Samling, p. 55: Københavns Museum.